Fondue Cookbook

Make These Sensational Fondue Recipes for Your Next Parties

By: Logan King

Edition Notice

The author has taken any step to make sure this book is accurate and safe. Every info is checked. However, every step you take following the book do it with caution and on your own accord.

If you end up with a copied and illegal version of this book please delete it and get the original. This will support the author to create even better books for everyone. Also, if possible report where you have found the illegal version.

Table of Contents

Introduction

Is there anything better than the fondue recipes compilation for the fondue lovers out there? These great-tasting recipes for fondue will make you want to have more and more! Make these recipes and entertain your taste buds this fall!

The ingredients used in this book are simple and can be easily found near your stores. Only a few preparation moments and just some items will lead to a wonderful fondue. If you use these recipes in a contest, you are definitely going to win. Doubt us? Try these recipes and tell us how much you liked this wide range of fondues. Everyone, including you, would want to dive just right in!

Recipe - 1 Orange Chocolate fondue

This Orange Chocolate Fondue recipe will make your day more special, invite your friends and family to this fondue party, take a dip and enjoy its mesmerizing taste.

Cooking time: 15 minutes

Serving size: 1-1/3 cups

Ingredients:

- Chocolate chip milk ½ cup
- Chopped bittersweet chocolate 3 ounces
- Whipping heavy cream ½ cup
- Thawed concentrate orange juice 3 tablespoons
- Cubed and thawed pound cake 1 frozen (16 ounces)
- Fresh assorted fruits

Instructions:

Take a heavy saucepan, combine and add both cream and chocolates.

Stir and cook it on low heat until it gets smooth.

Cook and stir orange concentrate juice and keep it warm.

Now serve it with your delicious cake and fruit.

Enjoy your yummiest chocolate orange fondue.

Recipe – 2 Beer and Cheddar fondue

This yummiest beer and the combination of cheddar fondue will make a perfect recipe. You can enjoy it with different fruits like apples, also with carrots chunks, bread cubes, and mushrooms, celery. Now today, you will make it and enjoy it with your loved ones.

Cooking time: 15 minutes

Serving size: 2 cups

Ingredients:

- Cheddar cheese shredded 4 cups
- All-purpose flour 1 tablespoon
- Nonalcoholic beer or beer 1 cup
- Minced garlic cloves 3
- Ground mustard 1-1/2 teaspoons
- Ground coarsely pepper ¼ teaspoon
- Radishes, breadsticks, and apple slice as you like

Instructions:

Take a large bowl, add and combine flour and cheese.

Take a small saucepan, now heat the garlic, pepper, mustard, and beer on medium flame until it gets smooth, and around the sides of the pan, the bubble will emerge.

Now let's slow down the heat on medium-low flame, put a handful of the mixture of cheese.

Cook and stir it constantly, until it gets completely smooth and melted.

Constantly add a mixture of cheese and remember to put 1 handful only at a time.

Give some time to cheese until it gets completely melt while adding the ingredients.

Keep it warm and serve it with radish, breadstick, and sliced apples.

Now serve the fondue to your folks and enjoy.

Recipe – 3 Pizza Fondue

This amazing and super quick recipe takes less than half an hour time to ready, now make this pizza fondue recipe and share it with your friends.

Cooking time: 20 minutes

Serving size: 6

Ingredients:

- Spaghetti meatless sauce 1 jar of 26 ounces
- Mozzarella shredded cheese 1 package of 8 ounces
- Parmesan grated cheese ¼ cup
- Dried oregano 2 teaspoons
- Minced dried onion 1 teaspoon
- Garlic salt ¼ teaspoon
- Cubed French bread 1 loaf of 16 ounces

Instructions:

Take a heavy saucepan, stir and cook mozzarella cheese, spaghetti sauce, oregano, parmesan cheese, garlic salt, and dried onion altogether.

Now slow down the heat to medium and stir it until the sauce and cheese become melt.

Now serve it with the French bread with cube shape for dipping.

Enjoy this amazing fondue.

Recipe - 4 Sensational Crabmeat Fondue

This crabmeat fondue makes a perfect combination of cheese and crabmeat. This fondue will surely give the perfect taste for your loved ones that how to being together and enjoy each bite of fondue with love.

Cooking time: 30 minutes

Serving size: 8 cups

Ingredients:

- Cubed butter ½ cup
- Finely chopped green onion 3
- Coarsely chopped imitation crabmeat 2 packages of 8 ounces
- Whole milk 2 cups
- Chicken broth or white wine ½ cup
- Pepper ¼ teaspoon
- Monterey jack shredded cheese 2 cups
- Swiss shredded cheese 2 cups
- Shredded Gruyere or add swiss shredded cheese 2 cups
- Process cubed cheese 1 cup (Velveeta)
- French bread cubed

Instruction:

Take a 6-qt stockpot on a medium-high flame, cook the butter, and stir it until it gets tender.

Now add crabs and cook them for 1-3 minutes until or longer and until heated through.

Stir and cook milk, pepper, and wine heat it until from the sides of the pan it gets bubbles.

Now slow down the heat to medium-low, add Monterey jack ½ cup of the cheese; stir and cook it until it gets completely melted.

For the sauces, constantly add the cheese at a time, only ½ cup; it will take time to get properly melted between every cheese addition you make.

Stir and cook until the mixture becomes smooth and thickened.

Now transfer the mixture to a fondue heated pot, and keep the mixture to bubble gently.

Now take a bread cube and serve it with the yummiest fondue.

Enjoy your fondue.

Recipe – 5 Mexican fondue

The recipe has the creamy texture of the fondue. It's a quick recipe for your guests and makes perfect and delicious fondue, its item is canned goods you can easily buy it and all the works are hands-on the cooker so let's try it today!

Cooking time: 15 minutes

Serving Size: 4-1/2 cups

Ingredients:

- Corn cream 1 can of 14-3/4 ounces
- Diced and drained tomatoes 1 can of 14-1/2 ounces
- Green chilies chopped 3 tablespoons
- Chili powder 1 teaspoon
- Process cubed cheese (Velveeta) 1 package of 16 ounces
- Cubes of French bread

Instruction:

Take a small bowl, add and combine tomatoes, corn, chili powder, and green chiles cook and stir it into cheese.

Put out the mixture into a 1-1/2 qt slow cooker, coat it with cooking oil spray to grease.

Cook and cover it on high until cheese becomes completely melted, for 1-1/2 hours, and stir it up every after 30 minutes.

Now serve it warm with cube shape bread.

Enjoy it with family and friends to have delightful moments.

Recipe - 6 Chocolate chipotle fondue

Here is an amazing fondue for the chocolate lover once you make it you will love this recipe, the easiest and quick recipe for your birthday parties. Make it and celebrate every important moment of life with these tasty fondues.

Cooking time: 11 minutes

Serving size: 3-1/4 cups

Ingredients:

- Chopped sweet dark baking bar chocolate 4 (4 ounces)
- Whipping cream 1 ½ cups
- Dulce de leche canned ½ cup
- Ground chile chipotle powder 1 teaspoon
- Liqueur coffee 1/3 cup
- Candied fruit dippers (you can add mango slice, pineapple, papaya strips, banana slice, pound cubes cake, marshmallows)

Instruction:

Take a medium saucepan add and combine 1 to 3 ingredients, stir and cook it constantly on medium-low heat until the chocolate becomes smooth and gets melted.

Now stir the chile powder and liqueur of coffee.

Put out the mixture of chocolate in a fondue, now keep it on the fondue burner.

Now serve it with tasty candied fruit, cake cubes, marshmallows, and banana slices as dippers.

Make it, dip it, and enjoy each bite of your fondue.

Recipe - 7 Caramel apple Fondue

This one recipe is an amazing healthy appetizer that makes you healthy and it's full of nutrition. The mixture of caramel with apple slices makes your meal more delicious.

Cooking time: 25 minutes

Serving size: 3-1/2 cups

Ingredients:

- Cubed butter ½ cup
- Brown sugar packed 2 cups
- Condensed sweetened milk 1 can of 14 ounces
- Corn light syrup 1 cup
- Water 2 tablespoons
- Vanilla extract 1 teaspoon
- Apple slices as you like

Instruction:

Take a heavy saucepan of 3-qt, add and combine the brown sugar, butter, corn syrup, water, and milk; bring it to boil on medium heat.

Cook and stir it for 8 to 10 minutes and until a thermometer dipped reads 230 degrees.

Now keep it away from heat and stir it in vanilla.

Transfer it to a small pot of fondue or 1-1/2- qt slow cooker.

Keep it warm and serve it with apple slices.

Recipe — 8 Best formula Three- Cheese Fondue

Ever you try a combination of three cheese formulas? Not yet? So here is a delicious fondue recipe for the cheese lover. Let's try this one recipe and share it with loved ones.

Cooking time: 20 minutes

Serving size: 24

Ingredients:

- White wine 1 cup
- Butter 1 tablespoon
- All-purpose flour 1 tablespoon
- Cubed Gruyere cheese 7 ounces
- Sharp cubed cheddar cheese 7 ounces
- Emmentaler cubed cheese 7 ounces

Instruction:

Take a small saucepan, put it in wine, and bring it to a boil.

After this, take a medium saucepan melt the butter in low-medium heat.

Now whisk it into the flour, cook, and stir it for 5 minutes, stirring it continuously to avoid burning and sticking.

When the flour becomes cooked, stir up the wine in the flour mixture smoothly.

Now whisk it until the mixture becomes smooth.

Now side by side, add the cubes of cheddar, Emmentaler, and gruyere cheese; stir it until the cheese becomes melts.

After this, put it into the fondue pot.

Keep it warm on a low flame.

Make it now and enjoy your delicious fondue.

Recipe – 9 Asparagus Glazed with white truffle fondue

This amazing and delicious asparagus glazed with truffle fondue make the perfect combination together. Make it as an appetizer or a side dish it's of your choice.

Cooking time: 15 minutes

Serving size: 6

Ingredients

- Unsalted butter 2 tablespoons (1 ounce)
- Minced shallots 2 tablespoons
- Thin- pencil asparagus 1 pound
- Salt and ground freshly pepper
- White fondue truffle ¼ cup (from 3.5 ounces jar)
- Minced tarragon 1 teaspoon

Instruction:

Before starting the fondue, heat up the oven and keep the position of the rack in the oven 8 inches away from the heat.

Take a large skillet and melt the butter, now add minced shallots; cook it over on medium-high heat till now it gets softens for 1 minute.

Now add seasoning of pepper and salt, asparagus, and cook it over on medium heat.

Stir it side by side until it gets crispy and lightly brown for 5 minutes.

Put the asparagus into a medium-size gratin dish, now spread the fondue truffle over them.

Boil it until it gets bubble and golden brown, shifting this dish for browning just for 1 minute.

Now serve and sprinkle it with the tarragon.

Recipe- 10 Totally Groovy Chocolate Fondue

This is a superb, quick, and yummiest groovy fondue recipe. It is simply and prepared in just 10 minutes; what are you waiting for, make it and serve it with your favorite snacks and fruits, now share with your loved ones.

Cooking time: 10 minutes

Serving Size: 6

Ingredients:

- Chocolate chips milk 2 cups
- Heavy cream 3 tablespoons
- Cherry brandy 2 tablespoons
- Brewed strong coffee 1 tablespoon
- Ground cinnamon 1/8 teaspoon

Instruction:

Add and combine cream, chocolate, brandy, coffee, and cinnamon. Put it in a fondue pot on a low flame or heat.

Cook it until it gets melt and stir it occasionally.

Now serve it with the combination of love and happiness.

Recipe — 11 Cheese lover fondue

This recipe will be best for cheese lovers. Let's try this one recipe, share it with your friends, and give them a special cheesy treat.

Cooking time: 15 minutes

Serving size: 2 cups

Ingredients

- Cornstarch divided 4 teaspoons
- White dry wine 1 tablespoon + 1 cup (divided)
- Gruyere shredded cheese 1-1/2 cups
- Swiss shredded cheese 1-1/2 cups
- Halved and peeled, garlic clove 1
- Lemon juice 1-1/2 teaspoons
- Garlic powder 1/8 teaspoon
- Dried oregano 1/8 teaspoon
- Worcestershire sauce 1/8 teaspoon
- Pepper hot sauce 3 drops
- Smoked miniature sausages, pretzels, and dill pickles

Instruction:

Take a small bowl, combine and add cornstarch 2 teaspoons with the wine of 1 tablespoon, and keep it aside.

Now combine leftover cornstarch and cheese and keep it aside.

Take a clove of garlic and cut it from the mid, now rub it into the large saucepan, and after this, discard this garlic.

Add leftover wine to the pan and cook it on medium heat until the bubbles emerge from the sides of the pan.

Now stir lemon juice into it.

Slow down the heat to medium-low and add the handful of the mixture of cheese.

Stir it continuously until the cheese becomes melts.

Constantly add the cheese; only one time add a handful of cheese; give some time to cheese that it gets completely melt.

Stir in the powder of garlic, Worcestershire sauce, pepper sauce, and oregano.

Now stir up the cornstarch mixture, add to the pan gradually.

Stir and cook until the mixture becomes smooth and thickened.

Keep the fondue warm, serve it with the miniature sausages, pretzels, and dill pickles.

Now serve it and share it with the cheese lovers.

Recipe – 12 Chocolate-Caramel Fondue

This chocolate caramel fondue is a special recipe for chocolate lovers, make this recipe and share it with your friends, and your kids will love this recipe. Let's make it and enjoy your vacation.

Cooking time: 10 minutes

Serving size: 2-1/2 cups

Ingredients:

- Condensed sweetened milk 1 can of 14 ounces
- Topping caramel ice cream 1 jar of 12 ounces
- Chopped unsweetened chocolate 3 ounces
- Fresh assorted fruits or Pretzels

Instruction:

Take a small saucepan, add and combine the milk, caramel, and chocolate topping.

Stir and cook it on low heat until it gets completely blended.

Transfer it into a warm fondue pot, and keep it warm.

Now serve it with fruits and pretzels and use it for dipping.

Recipe – 13 Mocha Fondue

This one mocha fondue recipe takes less than half-hour to get ready, make it for your family, and enjoy the little bit happiest moments with your family.

Cooking time: 20 minutes

Serving Size: 10

Ingredients:

Chocolate chips semisweet 2 cups

Cubed butter ¼ cup

Whipping heavy cream 1 cup

Brewed strong coffee 3 tablespoons

Salt 1/8 teaspoon

Lightly beaten, egg yolks 2 large

Sliced banana, cubed shape pound cake, and pineapple chunks, and fresh strawberries

Instruction:

Take a heavy saucepan, combine and add the 1 to 5 ingredients, stir and cook on medium flame until the chips become melted.

Now keep it aside from the heat, take a small bowl and put some amount of this mixture in egg yolks, and then put all of it into the pan.

Now mix it constantly, stir and cook until the thermometer reading becomes 160 degrees.

After this, transfer it into the fondue pot and keep it warm.

Serve the fondue with fruits and cake.

Recipe – 14 Fun-do Fondue

You should make this recipe and try to have some fun and enjoy it with your friends. This fondue is a quick and yummy recipe for your breakfast with a loaf of bread and slices of fruits and vegetables.

Cooking time: 20 minutes

Serving size : 3 cups

Ingredients:

- Jarlsberg shredded cheese 2 cups
- Swiss shredded cheese ½ cup
- All-purpose flour ¼ cup
- Ground mustard ½ teaspoon
- Ground freshly pepper ½ teaspoon
- Whipping heavy cream 1 cup
- Chicken broth reduced sodium 1 cup
- Honey 1 tablespoon
- Lemon juice 1 teaspoon
- Sliced pears, French cubed bread, and fresh assorted vegetables

Instruction:

Take a small bowl, combine, and add the 1 to 5 ingredients.

Take a saucepan, add and combine broth, cream, and honey, cook it until it gets to a boil, and stir it continuously.

Now slow down the heat on low medium and add a cheese mixture of ½ cup, stir and cook it until it gets completely melted.

Now constantly add the cheese at one time, only ½ cup.

Take some time for the cheese to get completely melt.

Stir and cook it constantly until it becomes smooth and thickened; now, stir up the lemon juice.

Transfer it into a fondue heated pot, keep the fondue gently bubbling.

Now serve it with the vegetables, pieces of bread, and pears for dipping.

If fondue looks too thick, then you can stir up the little broth more in it.

Recipe - 15 Bread Pot Fondue

This bread pot fondue recipe will make your day, make it on a special event as a starter and enjoy the cheesy, creamy, and spicy texture. This is an amazing and delicious way to serve your guests.

Cooking time: 1 hr. 30 minutes

Serving size: 32

Ingredients:

- Round loaf bread 1 (1 pound)
- Cheddar shredded cheese 1 package of 8 ounces
- Cream cheese 2 packages of 3 ounces
- Sour cream 1-1/2 cups
- Diced cooked ham 1 cup
- Green onion chopped ½ cup
- Green peppers chile diced 1 can of 4 ounces
- Worcestershire sauce 1 teaspoon
- Vegetable oil 2 tablespoons
- Melted butter 1 tablespoon

Instruction:

Before starting the fondue, heat the oven to 350F. From the top of the bread, cut it into a circle shape.

Now remove the top of the bread loaf and keep it aside, reserving the rest of the bread as dipping.

Take a medium bowl; now mix up the cream cheese, cheddar cheese, ham, sour cream, chile green pepper, green onion, and Worcestershire sauce.

In the bread bowl, put a spoon in it.

Take a foil paper and wrap the bowl lightly, and now put it on a baking sheet.

Transfer it to the oven and bake it until cheese becomes bubbly and melt for 1 hour.

After this, take the rest of the bread and cut it into slices shape.

Toss it with the melted butter and oil and keep it on the baking sheet.

Toast it into the oven until it becomes golden brown in 10 to 15 minutes.

Now serve your amazing fondue with the golden brown toast.

Recipe – 16 Slow – cooker Key Lime Fondue

This superb quick recipe and its preparation are just in 5 minutes. Let's make it and make your meal more healthy and full of creamy. Serve it with amazing fruits and crackers.

Cooking time: 50 minutes

Serving size: 3 cups

Ingredients:

- Condensed sweetened milk 1 can of 14 ounces
- Finely chopped baking white chocolate 12 ounces
- Lime regular juice or key lime ½ cup
- Lime zest grated 1 tablespoon
- Macaroon cookies, graham crackers, bananas ripe sliced, and fresh strawberries.

Instruction:

Take 1-1/2 qt slow cooker, add and combine white chocolate, milk, and lime juice.

Cover the cooker and cook on low flame for 50 to 60 minutes and until the chocolate becomes melted.

Stir up the zest of lime.

Now serve it with cookies, graham crackers, and fruits.

Make it and enjoy.

Recipe – 17 Shrimp Fondue

This quickest recipe of delicious shrimp fondue recipe will make your day. Make it for your guests and serve it with amazing garnishing and with fresh French bread. Everyone will ask to share this quick recipe with them.

Cooking time: 10 minutes

Serving size: 7

Ingredients:

- Sour cream 1 container of 16 ounces
- Cream cheese 1 package of 8 ounces
- Shrimp soup of condensed cream 1 can of 10.75 ounces
- Worcestershire sauce 1 dash
- Garlic salt 1 pinch

Instruction:

Take a pot of medium size, add cream cheese, sour melt cream, Worcestershire sauce, shrimp sauce, and garlic salt on low heat.

Cook it until it becomes melted together, and the mixture texture becomes creamy.

Now take a serving bowl and pour the fondue in it.

Serve it warm and enjoy this quick fondue.

Recipe – 18 Voodoo Fondue

This voodoo fondue recipe is an amazing way to present your dish with fruits and vegetables. Its mixture with cheese becomes more attractive and tasty. Make it and enjoy the yummiest fondue.

Cooking time: 30 minutes

Serving size: 8

Ingredients:

- White dry wine 1-1/2 cups
- Crushed garlic clove 1 large
- Shredded Swiss cheese 2 cups of 6 ounces
- Gruyere shredded 1 cup of 3 ounces
- Shredded Monterey jack 1 cup of 3 ounces
- Flour 2-1/2 tablespoons
- Chambord or kirsch 2 tablespoons (optional)
- Cayenne pepper 1/8 teaspoon
- Nutmeg 1/8 teaspoon
- Salt and pepper
- Prosciutto sliced 2 ounces
- Apples (wedges shape cutting) 3
- Pumpernickel bread 8 slices
- Red grapes 1 bunch
- Green grapes 1 bunch
- Cauliflower 1 head

Instructions:

Take a medium saucepan, add garlic and wine and bring it to boil until it becomes reduced to 1 cup.

On medium heat, simmer it for 1 minute.

Toss flour with cheese.

Add wine gradually and whisk it 1 scant cup at one time.

Now whisk it continuously before adding more of it as firstly, the cheese should be completely melted.

Add liqueur and also add nutmeg and cayenne, season with pepper and salt.

Cook it on low-medium heat until it becomes smooth and thickened in around 2 minutes.

Transfer it to a warm fondue pot and keep it warm.

For making the apple mummies, wrap the strips of prosciutto around the apple.

To make bat bread, cut it into bat shapes from the bread.

Take grapes and combine them for making eyeballs.

For making a blanched brain cut and blanch the florets of cauliflower.

Keep the cheese warm and serve it as you want to eat.

Recipe – 19 Beef and Beer Fondue

This special beef and beer fondue recipe is for meat lovers. You must try this recipe to make a new way to eat the healthy and tasty meatball fondue. Now let's make it today and make everyone in awe of your cooking skills.

Cooking time: 5 hours and 10 minutes

Serving size: 12

Ingredients:

- Ketchup 1 bottle of 32 ounces
- Beer 1 bottle or can of 12 fluid ounces
- Worcestershire sauce 1 teaspoon
- Bay leaves 2
- Ground lean beef 1-1/2 pounds 80%

Instructions:

Take a slow cooker, now add and mix up the ketchup, Worcestershire sauce, beer, and bay leave altogether now set it over high.

Make a meatball of ground beef, and take a skillet and cook meatballs on high medium heat. Stir it until it gets browned in around 7 minutes.

Now put these meatballs into a slow cooker.

For making the sauce thick, cook it on high heat for around 5 hours.

Before the serving, remove the leaves of the bay.

Now serve it warm and enjoy your beef beer fondue.

Recipe – 20 Peanut Butter Fondue

If you are eager to make something new and healthy today to keep your hunger at bay, here is the best and quick recipe for peanut butter fondue. Make it in a winter vacation and enjoy it with your loved ones.

Cooking time: 10 minutes

Serving size: 6

Ingredients:

- Brown sugar ¼ cup
- Corn light syrup ¼ cup
- Butter 2 tablespoons
- Peanut butter ½ cup
- Evaporated milk ½ cup
- Marshmallows 4 large
- Vanilla extract 1 teaspoon

Instruction

Take a small saucepan, cook, and stir the corn syrup, brown sugar, and butter together on low heat until the butter becomes melted.

Combine the mixture for around 5 minutes.

Now add evaporated milk, marshmallows, peanut butter into the mixture.

Cook and stir it continuously for 3 to 5 minutes more until the marshmallows become melted and its texture becomes smooth.

Now add the vanilla extract into the mixture of peanut butter.

After this, keep it aside from the heat.

Transfer it into a fondue pot.

Serve it and enjoy it with your family.

Recipe - 21 Cheese and Tomatoes Fondue

Have you ever try the fondue of tomatoes and cheese? If no then here we a superb quick delicious recipe of fondue. You must try this delicious and healthy food for your family members.

Cooking time: 20 minutes

Serving size: 24

Ingredients:

- Butter 2 tablespoons
- Minced garlic cloves 2
- Minced onion ½ teaspoon
- Chopped and seeded small tomatoes 3
- White dry wine 1-1/2 cups
- Gruyere shredded cheese 1 pound
- Swiss shredded cheese ½ pound

Instruction:

Take a double boiler or a fondue pot, add butter, and put it on medium heat until it gets melt.

Stir and cook the onion and garlic, gradually stir and cook until vegetables become soft.

Now add the tomatoes and cook it for more than 3 minutes.

Now pour the wine into the mixture.

Stir it continuously until the wine comes to boiling.

After this, keep this pot aside from the heat and stir the swiss and Gruyere cheese until it gets melt.

Now serve it and enjoy your tomatoes and cheese yummiest fondue.

Recipe - 22 Beef Tenderloin Fondue

This recipe is the quickest. It takes only 15 minutes, and your delicious fondue becomes ready. Now, what are you waiting for? Invite your friend and make a healthy beef tenderloin fondue for them.

Cooking time: 15 minutes

Additional: 4 hours

Serving size: 2

Ingredients:

- Soy sauce ¼ cup
- Worcestershire sauce 1 tablespoon
- Minced garlic clove 1 small
- Beef tenderloin 1-1/4 pounds (cut into cubes of ½ - inch)
- Vegetable broth 1 container (32 fluid ounce)
- Red dry wine ½ cup
- Chopped green onion 3

Instruction:

Take a plastic resealable bag and add soy sauce, garlic, and Worcestershire sauce, and also add cubes of beef and again seal this bag.

Put it flat into the refrigerator for 4 hours minimum, turn it side by side.

Now take the paper towel, and remove beef from the marinade and dry it with a pat.

After this, take a fondue pot, pour the vegetable broth in it, and heat it to 225 degrees f (105 degrees C).

Now add green onion and wine for simmering broth.

For dipping the cubes of beef, use the fondue forks and dip into the broth until it gets cooked for 1 -2 minutes for each forkful.

Now serve it with an amazing garnishing.

Recipe – 23 French Ham Cheese and Egg Fondue Casserole

This fresh ham cheese and its combination with egg make an amazing texture of fondue. Let's try it today to make your lunch more different and delicious.

Cooking time: 1 hour

Serving size: 12

Ingredients:

- Softened butter 2 tablespoons
- All-purpose flour 3 tablespoons
- Mustard powder 1 tablespoon
- Fully cubed cooked ham 3 cups
- Cubed cheddar cheese 8 ounces
- French bread day old cubed 3 cups
- Beaten eggs 4
- Milk 3 cups
- Pepper hot sauce 1 dash
- Melted butter 3 tablespoons
- Parmesan freshly grated cheese ½ cup

Instruction:

Take a glass baking dish of 9x13 inches, now grease it generously with melted butter.

Cook and stir mustard powder and flour together.

Take a big bowl for mixing, place cheddar cubes and ham in it, sprinkle it with the mixture of flour, and toss to coat it evenly.

Now add and toss these bread cubes to mix.

Take a separate bowl, whisk eggs, pepper hot sauce, and milk together.

Now take that prepared dish of baking, pour the bread mixture 1/3 part and place it out smoothly as a layer.

Drizzle it with butter 1 tablespoon, and sprinkle the parmesan cheese by 1/3 part.

Repeat the same procedure and making three layers.

Over the top, pour the mixture of egg, cover it with a plastic wrap sheet.

Now keep it in the refrigerator for 8 hours or overnight.

The next morning, put it out from the refrigerator, remove the plastic wrap, and keep it at room temperature for 30 minutes.

Before starting, heat the oven to 350 degrees F (175 degrees C)

Uncover it and bake in the oven until the egg becomes set and its top color becomes changes to golden brown and also crispy for 1 hour.

Now it's time to serve it your delicious fondue.

Recipe – 24 Toffee Fondue

This recipe makes an interesting way to make toffee fondue. You can make it for a kid's party or just to please your own inner child.

Cooking time: 3 hours

Serving size: 6 cups

Ingredients:

- Butter ¾ cup (pieces)
- Light brown sugar firmly packed 2 cups
- Corn light syrup 1-1/4 cups
- Water 3 tablespoons
- Condensed sweetened milk 2 cans of 14 ounces
- Toffee bits almond ¾ cup
- Vanilla extract 2 teaspoons
- Pear slices as you like
- Pretzel rods as you like
- Shortbread sticks as you like

Ingredients:

Take a slow cooker of 4 – quart and combine 1 to 5 ingredients.

Cook and cover on low heat for 3 hours. Stir it occasionally until it becomes smooth.

Now stir in the vanilla and toffee bits

Serve it with pear slices, short breadsticks, and pretzels rods.

Now serve with the yummiest toffees.

Recipe - 25 Chocolate Almond fondue

This chocolate fondue will make a healthy and full of nutrition fondue because the texture and combination of almond and chocolate make a delicious meal for us. Let's make it today and invite your friends.

Cooking time: 24 minutes

Serving size: 2 cups

Ingredients:

- Chopped unsweetened chocolate 8 ounces

- Condensed sweetened milk 1 can of 14 ounces

- Almond liqueur 3 tablespoons

- Salt 1/8 teaspoon

- Dippers: artisan marshmallows, apple slices, pound cake cubed, strawberries

Instruction:

Take a heavy saucepan, add and combine condensed milk, chocolate on low heat.

Stir and cook it continuously until it gets smooth and melted.

Now keep it aside from heat and stir in salt and liqueur.

Pour it out in a warm fondue pot, and heat it on a low flame.

Now serve it with a dipper of your choice.

Eat it and enjoy your fondue.

Recipe – 26 lemon Fondue

This lovely fondue makes a delicious texture and a sunshine sauce effect, make it and invite your special guests, and believe us, you are going to get a lot of compliments.

Cooking time: 15 minutes

Serving size: 5 cups

Ingredients:

- Sugar 1 cup
- Cornstarch ½ cup
- Salt ½ teaspoon
- Water 4 cups
- Cubed butter ½ cup
- Lemon juice ½ cup
- Grated zest of lemon 2 tablespoons
- Gingerbread, strawberries, and bite-sized meringues

Instruction:

Take a large and heavy saucepan, now add and combine the cornstarch, sugar, and salt.

Stir and cook it into the water until it gets smooth.

Cook and stir it on medium heat until it gets to a boil. To make it thickened, cook it for 1-2 minutes.

Now keep it aside from the heat, and stir in the butter, lemon juice, and zest of lemon until butter becomes melted.

Transfer it into a fondue pot and keep it warm.

Now serve and enjoy your fondue with gingerbread, strawberries, and meringues.

Recipe – 27 Thai Coconut Lime Fondue

This is one of the yummiest coconut lime fondues represent as a two-course meal. You can eat it with the dippers or with crackers and also make it soup texture while adding the hot rice and cook for just 1 minute and delicious and healthy meal is ready.

Cooking time: 50 minutes

Serving size: 6

Ingredients:

For Dippers:

- Pork tenderloin 1-1/2 pounds
- Cooking spray
- Water 1 tablespoon
- Rice vinegar 1 tablespoon
- Soy sauce low sodium 1 tablespoon
- Honey 1 tablespoon
- Snap peas sugar trimmed 2 cups

For Fondue:

- Sesame oil 1 teaspoon
- Peeled minced fresh ginger 1 tablespoon
- Minced garlic cloves 3
- Chicken broth less- sodium fat – free 1 can of 16 ounces
- All-purpose flour ¼ cup
- Water ¼ cup
- Coconut light milk 1 cup
- Lime grated rind 1 teaspoon
- Brown sugar 1-1/2 tablespoons
- Salt 1/8 teaspoon
- Red pepper crushed 1/8 teaspoon

Remaining ingredients

- Cooked hot rice 3 cups

Instructions:

Preheat the oven to 425 degrees.

For preparing a dipper, trim out fat from the pork.

Now take a cooking spray, coat the pork, take a roasting pan of the shallow bottom, and line with the foil.

Take a small bowl and then combine the vinegar, water, honey, and soy sauce; now brush up the mixture on the pork.

Now take a meat thermometer and put it inside the thickest part of pork, and make it at 425 degrees for 30 minutes, measure its reading up till to 160 degrees.

Now cut the pork into small cube pieces.

Now cook the peas in boiling water just for 1 minute until they get crispy tender. Now drain the water, then rinse it with chill water.

For making the fondue, take a medium saucepan on high medium heat; heat the oil.

Stir the garlic and ginger for 30 seconds.

Stir and cook in the broth. Cook it for 2 minutes until it gets to a boil.

Now keep it away from the heat and take a spoon of dry flour in a measuring cup, now maintain leveling it.

Add the water and flour and combine this mixture.

After this, add the mixture of flour, coconut milk, and the next five ingredients (from coconut milk to pepper).

Now cook this mixture on medium heat for 8 minutes or till it gets bubbly and slightly thick, and stirring frequently.

Take a fondue pot and pour the fondue in it.

Keep the fondue warm and serve it with peas and pork for dipping.

When you eat up with the dippers, now take a spoon of rice and cook it for 1 minute. And pour it out on the soup bowl.

Serve it.

Recipe – 28 White Chocolate Fondue

This fondue recipe seems the easiest way to serve a delicious meal to your unexpected guest and welcome and serve them with warm and healthy yummiest fondue.

Cooking time: 15 minutes

Serving size: 6

Ingredients

- Coarsely chopped white chocolate 12 ounces
- Heavy cream ¾ cup
- Vanilla extract ½ teaspoon
- Hulled strawberries 2 pints

Instruction:

Take a small heavy saucepan, now combine cream and chocolate.

Warm and cook it on low heat stir until the chocolate melts and the texture becomes smooth.

Transfer it into the fondue pot, stir up the vanilla and for dipping, serve it with strawberries.

Make it a quick recipe and enjoy the yummiest fondue.

Recipe – 29 Mocha Fondue

This mocha fondue recipe makes everyone curious to know its recipe. While they once taste this fondue easiest and quick meal for parties, there will be no leftovers. So make it today and get the praise you deserve.

Cooking time: 15 minutes

Serving size: 3 cups

Ingredients:

- Condensed milk sweetened 1 can of 14 ounces
- Chocolate morsels semisweet 1 package of 12 ounces
- Miniature marshmallows 1 cup
- Brewed strong coffee ¼ cup
- Kahlua or other liqueur flavored coffee 1/3 cup
- Cubes pound cakes as you like
- Angle cubes food cake as you like
- Pear and apple slices as you like

Instruction:

Take a medium saucepan, add and combine 1 to 4 ingredients on low-medium heat. Cook and stir it continuously until chocolate melts and its mixture becomes smooth.

Now stir it in Kahlua, take a fondue pot, and pour in it.

Put it on the fondue burner.

Serve it with fruits and cake cubes as a dipper.

Enjoy it to the fullest.

Recipe – 30 chocolate – Frangelico Fondue

This chocolate Frangelico fondue makes your day more special; its quick and thick texture makes everyone love this recipe, so make it today and share it with your chocolate lovers' friends.

Cooking time: 35 minutes

Serving size: 8

Ingredients:

- Half and half 1/3 cup
- Free-fat milk ¼ cup
- Chopped semisweet chocolate 8 ounces
- Sifted sugar powered 1-1/4 cups
- Corn syrup dark 2 tablespoons
- Frangelico 2 tablespoons
- Small quartered strawberries 2 cups

Instruction:

Take a medium saucepan, combine and add 1 to 3 ingredients, and cook and stir it on low heat until it gets a smooth texture.

Keep it stirring. After this, add in corn syrup and sugar.

Now cook it for 10 minutes until its texture becomes smooth, and stirring it constantly.

Stir it in a liqueur, take a fondue pot, and pour in it.

Keep it warm in a low flame.

Serve it with strawberries and cakes.

Conclusion

Cook all varieties of fondue recipes for your folks and friends and get praise for your cooking skills. Just make any of the meatball, pizza fondue, or white chocolate fondue or sauces dishes present in this cookbook, serve your family, and watch everyone get delighted because of the tasty flavor and exquisite aroma the sweet and spicy possesses.

All of the recipes are unique in their way. Some have the combination of Thai rice, lemon fondue, chocolate, and pizza fondue others have it with spices. Try all of these recipes to experience diverse varieties of tastes and especially the exquisite smell and textures. You can easily learn to cook by following the instructions in each recipe.

We hope you will try these recipes from this fondue recipes cookbook and make everyone happy and healthy.

May God grant you a healthy and prosperous life ahead.

Thank You.

About the Author

Since he was a child, Logan King enjoyed watching his mom cook. For him, it was even more fun than playing with his friends. That's how he fell in love with cooking. In fact, the first thing he ever cooked on his own was a cupcake, a surprise for his little sister, which not even his mom was expecting.

Now, supported by the whole family he is constantly sharing new recipes of his own creations. He finished a gastronomy academy when he was 18 and continued his career as a chef and recipe developer.

Now his goal is to educate and help people fell in love with cooking as he did. Actually, he is advising mothers and fathers to give their children an opportunity in the kitchen, because they never know, maybe their kid could be the next top chef.

Even though he pursued a career as a chef, his cookbooks are designed for everyone, with and without cooking experience. He even says, "even if you don't know where your knife is you will be able to do my recipes."

The gastronomy field is large and there is no end in the options, ingredient combinations, and cooking techniques. That's why he tries his best to keep his audience informed about the newest recipes, and even give them a chance to modify his recipes so that they can find a new one, one that they can call their own.

Appendices

I am not stopping with this book. There are going to a lot more so make sure you are ready for the amazing recipes that you will be able to get from me. You can always be sure that they are going to be simple and easy to follow.

But thank you for choosing my book. I know that you haven't made a mistake and you will realize that too, well, as soon as you start making the recipes.

Please do share your experience about the written as well as the practical part of this book. Leave feedback that will help me and other people, I'll greatly apricate this.

Thank you once more

Have a great adventure with my book

Yours Truly

Logan King

Made in the USA
Columbia, SC
13 December 2021